Bible
Word Search
Collection #12

BARBOUR
PUBLISHING, INC.
Uhrichsville, Ohio

© MCMXCVIII by Barbour Publishing, Inc.

ISBN 1-57748-373-1

All Scripture references are from the Authorized King James Version of the Bible.

Bonus Trivia questions are taken from *Church Challenge* by Marvin Hinten, published by Barbour Publishing, Inc., Uhrichsville, OH 44683.

Published by Barbour Publishing, Inc., P.O. Box 719, Uhrichsville, Ohio 44683 http://www.barbourbooks.com

Member of the
Evangelical Christian
Publishers Association

Printed in the United States of America.

Bible
Word Search
Collection #12

1

Priscilla Runyon

Centenarians

AARON	JOSHUA
ABRAHAM	LAMECH
ADAM	MAHALALEEL
ARPHAXAD	METHUSELAH
CAINAN	MOSES
EBER	NAHOR
ENOCH	NOAH
ENOS	PELEG
ISAAC	REU
ISHMAEL	SALAH
JACOB	SARAH
JARED	SERUG
JEHOIADA	SETH
JOB	SHEM
JOSEPH	TERAH

```
N X G C C J A C O B J M A D A
O A F R R O E D E R A J Z R A
A H H S E S I V B E O E P A R
H G D O H E D T C B R H E Z O
Z O P N R P G A B E A O L H N
L A M E C H A N P X J I E A M
E B O S A S K O A O S A G L G
E R S I I K O D L H R D C E V
L A E E N O C H M G O A R S Y
A H S R A X I A C J O S H U A
L A M R N L E V K J G E J H S
A M O E O L V H C Y U D A T A
H U F B H A R E T I R E U E R
A U Z U K S B X R E E Z T M A
M L P I K S P D W Z S A L A H
```

◇ **Bonus Trivia**

The Revised Standard Version of the Bible
has just under 1,000,000 words. Approxi-
mately how many words are in the Reader's
Digest condensed version?

600,000.

5

2

Priscilla Runyon

False Gods

ADRAMMELECH	GRAVEN IMAGE
ANAMMELECH	JUPITER
ASHERAH	MERCURY (HERMES)
ASHIMA	MERODACH
ASHTORETH	MOLECH
BAAL	MOON
BAAL-BERITH	NERGAL
BAAL-PEOR	NIBHAZ
BAAL-ZEBUB	NISROCH
BEL	PEOR
CHEMOSH	SATYRS
DAGON	TAMMUZ
DIANA (ARTEMIS)	TERAPHIM

6

```
Q V F C H C E L E M M A R D A
S S R Y T A S G D I L N L H N
N U Y W E J J T I H Z T K K A
E R O G R A U Y A S R O E P M
R O N O O M P C N O G A D L M
G E I I T G I Z A M I H S A E
A P S B H A T A W E C V S A L
L L R A S H E R A H Z L J B E
U A O A A R R L H C E L O M C
Z A C L L B A A L B E R I T H
U B H Z Z J H K M S W Z G F I
M N M E R O D A C H E K Z L P
M N I B H A Z Q O K O X B O R
A Y R U C R E M I H P A R E T
T V Y B E G A M I N E V A R G
```

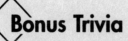

7

3

Yvonne Goodwin

Cities of the 12 Tribes

APHEK	HEBRON
ASHDOD	HESHBON
ASHKELON	HORMAH
BEERSHEBA	JABESH-GILEAD
BETHEL	JERICHO
BETHLEHEM	JOPPA
BETH-SHEMESH	KIRIATH-JEARIM
DIBON	MEGIDDO
GAZA	SHILOH
GEZER	SUCCOTH
GIBEON	TYRE
GOLAN	ZIKLAG
HAZOR	

```
H J N J Z A B E H S R E E B B
E O U C I H F J R R Y J N E E
B P R K K I Q E O R E K T M T
R P G M L M Z Z J Y L H W I H
O A J R A E A S A E S C Z R L
N C X R G H E A B H U O Q A E
O B E T H E L I E T C Q H E H
L K O R O H O M S A C Z N J E
E M K H L L E E H E O T D H M
K Y S E I S D H G T T Y Z T E
H H E S H B O N I J H R W A G
S W L B S P G Z L M A E W I I
A S H D O D A L E Z B I C R D
O H C I R E J N A L O G A I D
L K N O E B I G D I B O N K O
```

<svg diamond icon> **Bonus Trivia**

In the novel *In His Steps*, what four-word
phrase do the committed disciples
continually ask themselves?

What would Jesus do?

4

Lynn Wallace

Beginnings

ALTAR	MEN
ANIMALS	NATIONS
CURSE	PLANTS
DAY	REDEMPTION
DEVILTRY	SALVATION
DOGS	SEA
DRUNKENNESS	SIN
DRY LAND	SKY
FAMILY	SONS
FIRMAMENT	STARS
FORGIVENESS	SUN
FOWL	TREES
GRACE	VALES
HEAVENS	WATER
HOME	WAY
JUDGMENT	WHALES
LANGUAGES	WIFE
LIFE	WOMAN
LIGHT	WORLD
MARRIAGE	YOU
ME	

```
P  J  W  H  A  L  E  S  W  W  O  R  L  D  J
E  R  E  D  E  M  P  T  I  O  N  Y  O  U  E
F  A  N  A  T  I  O  N  S  M  M  A  D  C  F
I  L  B  N  E  M  A  L  T  A  R  G  A  S  A
L  S  A  L  V  A  T  I  O  N  M  R  S  E  M
W  I  F  E  S  R  A  T  S  E  G  S  Q  H  I
O  H  E  A  V  E  N  S  N  S  E  E  R  T  L
F  A  W  A  T  E  R  T  S  N  O  S  S  K  Y
D  R  Y  L  A  N  D  D  E  L  I  G  H  T  R
S  L  A  M  I  N  A  V  A  L  E  S  A  P  T
E  S  R  U  C  F  I  R  M  A  M  E  N  T  L
S  U  N  D  O  G  S  S  T  N  A  L  P  N  I
D  A  Y  D  R  U  N  K  E  N  N  E  S  S  V
M  A  H  O  M  E  E  G  A  I  R  R  A  M  E
W  C  F  A  E  S  E  G  A  U  G  N  A  L  D
```

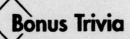

Bonus Trivia

What was Corrie ten Boom's honored nickname in Southeast Asia?

Double-old Grandmother.

5

Linda Amidon Pogue

A Seller of Purple
(Acts 16:13-15)

ABIDE	PRAYER
ATTENDED	PURPLE
BAPTIZED	RESORTED
BESOUGHT	RIVER SIDE
CERTAIN WOMAN	SABBATH
CITY	SELLER
CONSTRAINED	SPAKE
FAITHFUL	SPOKEN
HEART	THITHER
HOUSEHOLD	THYATIRA
JUDGED	WOMEN
LYDIA	WORSHIPPED
PAUL	

```
D E D N E T T A R I T A Y H T
T M L F J F A I T H F U L U H
C I T Y Q O Q U I X G Q R T G
Y I S A B B A T H L K N Z R U
D E E H U R H C Y E A L E L O
E L D K O E D D W M A L A T S
N P I Z R U I B O Z L R Y V E
I R S E Z A S W R E M G T S B
A U R P X B N E S L Z H V P A
R P E L K I S K H N G H A A P
T R V C A D G S I O N U X K T
S A I T N E K O P S L U U E I
N Y R T E K A C P A G D S O Z
O E S H L W O M E N E U K F E
C R E S O R T E D E G D U J D
```

Bonus Trivia

What is the meaning of "Maranatha," the word said at the end of many communion services in the early church?

"Our Lord, come."

6

Jayne Stratmeyer

The Lord Is My Shepherd
(Psalm 23)

LORD	DEATH
SHEPHERD	FEAR
MAKETH	NO EVIL
LIE	ROD
DOWN	STAFF
GREEN	COMFORT
PASTURES	PREPAREST
BESIDE	TABLE
STILL	HEAD
WATERS	OIL
RESTORETH	CUP
SOUL	RUNNETH
LEADETH	OVER
PATHS	DWELL
RIGHTEOUSNESS	HOUSE
WALK	FOR
VALLEY	EVER
SHADOW	

```
T  S  S  S  V  I  E  D  I  S  E  B  H  Q  L
A  H  T  H  K  B  G  W  T  V  A  L  L  E  Y
B  A  A  E  D  A  L  I  V  E  O  N  L  I  O
L  D  F  P  R  O  L  G  F  S  I  F  F  D  I
E  O  F  H  V  L  W  K  L  A  W  L  R  H  L
N  W  Y  E  R  M  M  N  G  S  F  O  R  L  E
P  E  R  R  V  E  A  J  H  O  L  E  H  D  A
R  A  E  D  K  E  S  K  C  U  P  R  A  T  D
E  D  S  R  W  N  R  T  E  L  Z  U  P  R  E
P  H  R  T  G  E  W  V  O  T  K  N  A  O  T
A  O  T  C  U  A  L  S  R  R  H  N  T  F  H
R  U  O  A  T  R  B  L  O  A  E  E  H  M  W
E  S  T  E  E  P  E  V  D  W  A  T  S  O  H
S  E  R  U  O  D  C  S  D  R  D  H  H  C  E
T  S  R  I  G  H  T  E  O  U  S  N  E  S  S
```

Bonus Trivia

Complete this Augustinian saying: Our hearts are restless. . .

"till they rest in Him." (sometimes phrased "till they rest in Thee").

7

Pam Powell

Heroes of Faith
(Hebrews 11)

ABEL	NOAH
ABRAHAM	PARENTS
BARAK	PERFECT
DAVID	PROMISE
ENOCH	PROPHETS
FAITH	RAHAB
GEDEON	REPORT
ISAAC	SAMSON
ISRAEL	SAMUEL
JACOB	SARA
JEPHTHAE	SCOURGINGS
JOSEPH	SLAIN
JOSHUA	SUBSTANCE
MOCKINGS	WANDERED
MOSES	WOMEN

```
M O C K I N G S Y R B O J C P
D R Z B O C A J H A L O U R P
T R B A H A R C R E S L O A E
A C A R A S O A U H E M R A E
S B E V I N K M U A I E H C B
G C R F E Q A A R S N T N W H
I E O A R S F S E T H A M D A
S R D U H E I T S P T A O E S
A S J E R A P U E S S H S R T
A T A O O G M J B J C A E E E
C Q R M S N I U D F Q O S D H
D Y E O S E S N E I A N L N P
N J Z B P O P X G I V I L A O
W O M E N E N H M S S A T W R
S L A I N E R F L E B A D H P
```

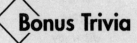

Bonus Trivia

What animal do the initial letters of "Jesus Christ, God's Son, Savior" spell in Greek?

Fish.

8

Pamela Jensen

Elisha

AX	MOAB
BARLEY	MOUNT
BETHEL	NAAMAN
BLINDNESS	OIL
BREAD	PEACE
BURIED	PLOWING
CARMEL	PRAY
CORN	PROPHET
DOUBLE	SAMARIA
ELIJAH	SEVEN
FAMINE	SHAPHAT
GOD	SICKNESS
HAZAEL	SNEEZED
HEALED	SON
ISRAEL	SPIRIT
JERICHO	SYRIA
JORDAN	VICTORY
LEPROSY	WATER
MAN	WEPT
MANTLE	WIDOW
MINISTERED	

```
S H A P H A T V B D O U B L E
B A R L E Y U S E V E N S U X
U S P I R I T R T Z W G S Y F
R V L N G R E O H C I R E J S
I C O W A T E R E B D F N L S
E S W I S R A E L T O O K E E
D E I I M N D P N B W L C M N
O L N R A E E U T I E C I R D
G I G M L A O E N A M Y S A N
M J A A C M H L Z M J A E C I
A A E E L P R A Y E O T F O L
N H U I O A H Q X O D A E R B
T J O R D A N A W E P T B N V
L E P R O S Y R O T C I V N V
E A I R A M A S Y R I A P A X
```

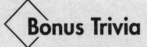

Bonus Trivia

What was William Booth's official title?

General of the Army (the Salvation Army,
that is).

9

D. Hittner

Hebrew Words in Psalms

AIJELETH SHAHAR	MAHALATH
ALAMOTH	MASCHIL
ALEPH	MICHTAM
BETH	NEGINAH
DALETH	NEGINOTH
EDUTH	NUN
GIMEL	RESH
GITTITH	SELAH
JEDUTHUN	SHIGGAION
KOPH	TAU
LAMED	TETH
LEANNOTH	

```
R  T  T  I  N  X  Y  G  Y  T  D  U  Q  S  L
O  A  S  P  B  G  I  M  E  L  B  J  O  S  I
U  U  H  L  K  U  Q  D  Z  B  E  N  C  P  M
N  O  I  A  G  G  I  H  S  D  D  E  B  V  I
U  H  S  W  H  I  H  W  F  U  G  M  E  C
N  T  Z  F  L  S  H  T  I  T  T  I  G  P  H
N  E  G  I  N  A  H  N  A  S  H  N  W  T  T
U  L  S  A  C  U  M  T  V  L  X  O  E  S  A
H  A  X  T  N  Q  I  E  E  L  A  T  X  Q  M
S  D  X  L  P  B  K  A  D  L  D  H  M  E  G
E  F  A  O  W  L  N  J  A  S  E  D  A  H  E
R  B  L  E  K  N  B  M  G  K  U  J  K  M  J
V  L  E  L  O  D  O  M  M  A  Y  F  I  N  F
Y  M  P  T  P  T  E  M  F  J  S  E  L  A  H
B  Y  H  E  H  T  M  M  A  S  C  H  I  L  Q
```

Bonus Trivia

What "Peanuts" character has the same name as a person in the New Testament?

Linus.

21

10

D. Hittner

Words from Ecclesiastes

ADVERSITY	PREACHER
BEGINNING	PROSPERITY
CHANCE	RIGHTEOUS
COMMANDMENTS	SINNER
FAVOR	SPIRIT
FEAR GOD	TIME
FOOLISH	UNDER THE SUN
INCREASE	UPRIGHT
JOY	VANITY
JUDGMENT	WISDOM
LABOUR	WORKS
PLEASURE	YOUTH
POWER	

```
U C V A N I T Y W I S D O M Z
N O X Q N G T E N T S E B E A
D M E S A E R C N I I P K D G
E M J L T X R U O B A L V U N
R A G R T I R E H C A E R P I
T N L O I S M L Y S R A J R N
H D Y V Z G I E T S I S U I N
E M A A J W H I I V W U D G I
S E D F B O Y T R E G R G H G
U N Y A P U Y Z E B V E M T E
N T U H L U F F P O B N E U B
Z S M F O O L I S H U W N O I
T I R I P S K R O W Y S T Y V
R E W O P D O G R A E F D T U
E C N A H C F Y P R E N N I S
```

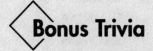

Bonus Trivia

What is the Septuagint?

The oldest translation of the Bible (the Hebrew Old Testament into Greek).

11

Judges & Leaders

D. Hittner

ABDON	JAMES
ABIAH	JEPHTHAH
ABIMELECH	JEREBOAM
ABRAHAM	JOEL
AHAB	JOSEPH
BARAK	JOSHUA
DANIEL	MOSES
DAVID	NEHEMIAH
DEBORAH	OTHNIEL
EHUD	PAUL
ELI	PETER
ELON	REHOBOAM
GIDEON	SAMSON
HEZEKIAH	SAMUEL
IBZAN	SHAMGAR
ISAAC	SOLOMON
JACOB	TOLA
JAIR	

```
O  T  H  N  I  E  L  K  A  N  Q  L  N  S  Z
R  J  A  W  H  W  S  B  E  H  C  M  O  A  R
D  W  I  R  N  P  I  H  N  A  A  L  E  M  H
I  J  K  J  A  M  E  S  A  O  O  B  D  U  A
V  B  E  I  E  M  A  S  B  M  D  B  I  E  B
A  W  Z  L  I  P  I  O  O  W  G  B  G  L  I
D  N  E  A  B  M  H  N  B  J  O  A  A  D  A
I  C  H  S  N  E  S  T  D  E  B  O  R  A  H
H  E  O  J  R  Z  M  A  H  A  R  B  A  N  H
B  L  A  J  I  O  A  U  M  A  E  E  O  I  L
Q  I  O  F  S  L  D  K  L  S  H  B  J  E  E
R  E  T  E  P  G  A  U  H  S  O  J  X  L  H
L  Y  S  J  X  R  A  M  F  C  B  N  O  F  R
Q  T  O  L  A  P  K  Q  A  P  D  N  L  H  P
B  D  S  B  N  I  P  J  F  T  G  D  M  E  H
```

◇ **Bonus Trivia**

What was the unusual occupation of Timothy Dwight, composer of "I Love Thy Kingdom, Lord"?

He was president of Yale University.

12

Creation

Jenny Steele

ADAM	GOD
BEGINNING	HEAVEN
CREATED	HIDDEKEL
DAY	MOON
EARTH	NIGHT
EDEN	PISON
EUPHRATES	SEASONS
EVE	SECOND
FIFTH	SEVENTH
FIRST	SIXTH
FOURTH	STARS
GARDEN	SUN
GENESIS	THIRD
GIHON	YEARS

```
F S T A R S X V V X N I G H T
O M F E F X B E G I N N I N G
U S I F A H M V S E V E N T H
R N F Y G R C F F I N L E I U
T D T I S R T X I Q F E B V S
H H H M E U P H R A T E S Q E
J O C A C G I E S M O A G I A
N J T P O T S A T P O C F U S
B E G Q N K O V A R L O M Y O
D E M Y D U N E Y V U C N P N
I I T S E R T N L E H A H E S
Z T H I D D E K E L A T D N N
T I I P A N E H V Q S R W A P
C N R S U V W N Q P A Z S R M
G O D S I X T H C G X D A Y O
```

Bonus Trivia

How many theses did Martin Luther nail up
for discussion to the Wittenberg Door?

95.

27

13

Brothers

Mary Ann Freeman

AARON	JAMES
ABEL	JAPHETH
ANDREW	JOHN
ASHER	JOSEPH
BENJAMIN	JUDAH
CAIN	LEVI
DAN	MANASSEH
EPHRAIM	MOSES
ESAU	NAPHTALI
GAD	PETER
HAM	PHINEHAS
HOPHNI	REUBEN
ISAAC	SETH
ISHMAEL	SHEM
ISSACHAR	SIMEON
JACOB	ZEBULUN

```
J R A H C A S S I R G Z C V W
A U I S H M A E L W L N Z F Z
P C D B F H N B E N J A M I N
H O A A I H A R H P E S O J U
E E G S H I D N J E W I L D L
T H J H S N L H O P H N I N U
H R Y E A P H R U E A T M S B
N E U R H C A A S I M Z E L E
J U A S E G O B L E V I E S Z
G B H E N K C A I N F B S D Y
S E K N I S T O X J A M E S O
E N Q O H H A M M I A R H P E
S U V R P E T E R E N C U C V
O J H A P M Q R B I N H O J Z
M A N A S S E H S R W G S B U
```

Bonus Trivia

To what creature does Jonathan Edwards compare sinners in his famous sermon, "Sinners in the Hands of an Angry God"?

A spider.

14

Mary Louise DeMott

Bible People Who Wept

ABRAHAM	JEWISH PEOPLE
BABY MOSES	JOB
BENJAMIN	JONATHAN
DAVID	JOSEPH
ELISHA	MELCHISEDEC
EPHESUS ELDERS	NAOMI
ESAU	ORPAH
EZRA	PETER
HAGAR	RACHEL
HANNAH	RUTH
HEZEKIAH	SAMSON'S WIFE
ISAIAH	SAUL
JACOB	TIMOTHY
JEREMIAH	WIDOW OF NAIN

```
H E A Y U M Y H T O M I T J M
E A P B E N J A M I N U A E B
Z J N H T U R I B J O B L V A
E J P N E J O S E P H C E U B
K P E A A S A U L K H L N V Y
I D T O M H U F Q I P A I M M
A M E M W P B S S O H M S A O
H H R I G O L E E T M U A H S
J A C N C E D P A L R A I A E
A I L A H E H N A A D S A R S
H M J C C S O I G Y Y E H B O
S E A J I J P A E Z R A R A R
I R E W A Y H B D I V A D S P
L E E W I D O W O F N A I N A
E J S A M S O N S W I F E S H
```

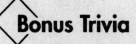

Bonus Trivia

How is the German phrase "Ein Feste Burg" generally translated into English?

A Mighty Fortress.

15

Mary Louise DeMott

Biblical Types and Foreshadows of Christ

ABRAHAM	JOSEPH
ADAM	JOSHUA
BULLOCK	LAMB
DANIEL	LION
DAVID	MELCHIZEDEK
DOVE	MOSES
EAGLE	NEHEMIAH
ELIJAH	NOAH
ELISHA	OX
EZEKIEL	PIGEON
EZRA	RAM
HEIFER	SCAPEGOAT
ISAAC	SERPENT
JEREMIAH	SHEEP
JONAH	SOLOMON

```
D O F Z O M A D A M T J E M D
J A N E H E M I A H X E E O A
E T V O S J X R N O I L V S N
R K P I N O A H V N C W T E I
E T I B D S P E E H S M H S E
M A G E U E Z L I S A A C J L
I O E L T P E Z S E R P E N T
A G O G T H E L I J A H Z K J
H E N A K D M F I M E V O D E
N P B E E A A G A S Z I X S A
B A G K H B X R L F H E H N U
M C J A S O L O M O N A Q A H
A S R E D R E F I E H K B R S
L B U L L O C K P K J W O Z O
A J O N A H X L E I K E Z E J
```

Bonus Trivia

With what hymn are Billy Graham Crusades usually associated?

"Just As I Am."

16

Faith Wade

Samson

ASHKELON	LOCKS
BEES	MANOAH
CORDS	NAZARITE
CORN	OLIVES
DAN	PHILISTINES
DELILAH	PILLARS
DOORS	RAMATH-LEHI
ENHAKKORE	RAZOR
ETAM	RIDDLE
EYES	ROPES
FEAST	SAMSON
FOXES	SHAVEN
GARMENTS	SLAUGHTER
GATE	SOREK
GAZA	SPIRIT
GRIND	STRENGTH
HONEY	TAIL
JAWBONE	TIMNATH
LEHI	WIFE
LION	ZORAH

```
S E V I L O S T N E M R A G R
C O R D S J N O L E K H S A A
S P S W Q H A R O Z B C L T M
E D I M A N O A H E S O A E A
S F E A S T O L E H I R U K T
E P S N E A D S T R E N G T H
N I E P P E T A M G T E H E L
I L X T O I V W N A M V T R E
T L O A R Q R A E Z S A E O H
S A F I R O Z A R A P H R K I
I R P L J A W B O N E S L K E
L S Z G R I N D O O R S E A Y
I N O I L O C K S O R E K H E
H W T I M N A T H O N E Y N S
P E L D D I R H H A L I L E D
```

Bonus Trivia

On what television show did ordained Southern Baptist minister Grady Nutt regularly appear?

"Hee-Haw" (as himself).

17

Faith Wade

Island of Cyprus

ASINE	NEAPAPHOS
CARPASIA	NEMESUS
CERMIA	PALOEA
CERYNIA	PALOEAPOLIS
CHYTRI	PALOEPAPHOS
CURIUM	PEGOE
ELOEA	SALAMIS
IDALIUM	SOLI
LAPETHUS	TAMASSUS
LEUCOLIA	THREMITHUS
LEUCOSIA	THRONI
MACARIA	URANIA
MARIUMARSINOE	VENERIS
MELABRUM	

```
S T V S O H P A P E O L A P M
C U R I U M H F X D U I X A E
E Q H S O H P A P A E N R L L
R C K T V E N E R I S I T O A
M Q Y E I I D A L I U M A E B
I A K P N M N C D M A B M A R
A I L O C U E L A E O L A P U
Y F R S E R A R O Q U L S O M
I H P N Y P S L H R U E S L A
T Z I N E I E A A T E U U I C
G S I T N S E N L A Q C S S A
A A H O N P I O Y A R O M O R
H U E N V A C T G T M S V W I
S O L I S U S E M E N I Y Q A
N M I R T Y H C A R P A S I A
```

◇ **Bonus Trivia**

If tradition is true, what was the chief difference in the crucifixions of Jesus and Peter?

Peter was crucified upside-down (he allegedly said he wasn't worthy to be crucified like Jesus).

18

Erin Wade

Esther

ABIHAIL	JEWS
AHASUERUS	MORDECAI
BANQUET	PALACE
BIGTHAN	PETITION
CROWN	QUEEN
DECREE	REQUEST
DELIVERANCE	RING
ESTHER	SCEPTRE
GALLOWS	SEAL
HADASSAH	SHUSHAN
HAMAN	TERESH
HARBONAH	VASHTI
HEGAI	ZERESH
HORSE	

```
F I Y U V S N A H T G I B S D
W H D Q D W T S E U Q E R E H
P I A T O I A B I H A I L A S
S T A R K H S E R E T I N L E
W H C L B M H E L P V E A E R
O S P H U O I A G E H R H C E
L A S R R R N H R T P T S A Z
L V I S G D N A H I P P U L H
A N E L W E N M H T O E H A T
G P S G H C H A H I C C S P E
A P T E E A A N S O F S N Z U
N C H L A I M X Q N A A E Y Q
S W E J E E R C E D K T E Y N
L J R M I Q W H A M O C U M A
S U R E U S A H A T J G Q M B
```

◇ Bonus Trivia

What group of people originally fought for the right to affirm in court rather than having to swear on a Bible?

Atheists.

39

19

Faith Wade

Peter

AENEAS	GALILEE
AFRAID	GETHSEMANE
ANDREW	HOUSETOP
ANGEL	JOPPA
ANTIOCH	JOURNEY
BOAT	LYDDA
CAESAREA	MALCHUS
CAPERNAUM	PRISON
COCK	RHODA
CORNELIUS	ROCK
DENY	SHEET
DISCIPLE	SIMON
DORCAS	SWORD
DOUBT	TABITHA
EAR	TIBERIAS
FISH	VISION
FISHERS	WALKED

```
O J D S P O T E S U O H S L R
K E E I K E A W G F D I A I Z
F T K M A R O N O I T A C E C
S S L O X R O M S M P A R D A
U U A N D I F C U P K X O D E
H I W I S N I A O C E T D B S
C L R I O P N J O A E Y Z N A
L E V S L R O C K H L N S S R
A N I E E U H A N T I O C H E
M R F P R V J O C I L G O E A
P O A N T B U O D B A E X E Y
S C E Y W E R D N A G N Y T N
H Y S A I R E B I T T W G O E
A E N E A S R E H S I F F E D
H S I F E N A M E S H T E G L
```

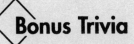

Bonus Trivia

For what is Anglican bishop William
Wilberforce most remembered?

He led the fight to abolish England's slave
trade.

20

Vicki Hicks

Solomon

ALTAR	PRAYER
ARK	QUEEN
BATHSHEBA	REHOBOAM
CEDAR	SACRIFICES
DAVID	SHEBA
DEDICATION	SOLOMON
FEAST	SPICES
GOLD	STONES
HEART	TABERNACLE
ISRAEL	TEMPLE
JUDGE	THRONE
KING	VESSELS
LEBANON	WISDOM
PALACE	WIVES

J	F	R	Q	S	E	N	O	T	S	D	A	V	W	P
S	U	W	A	H	C	T	S	A	E	F	C	I	P	H
E	R	D	C	D	A	Q	R	D	B	F	S	T	A	Z
C	S	Z	G	E	E	D	I	V	A	D	D	E	L	E
I	O	B	I	E	M	C	I	U	O	G	W	M	A	L
P	L	Q	A	F	A	Y	L	M	V	A	A	Q	C	C
S	O	R	A	T	L	A	O	E	B	O	R	U	E	A
W	M	R	I	G	H	I	S	E	B	N	K	E	O	N
R	O	O	I	E	L	S	H	O	Y	A	I	E	V	R
X	N	T	A	E	E	S	H	D	E	K	N	N	H	E
S	G	R	A	L	Y	E	Q	E	H	L	G	O	Q	B
E	T	R	S	V	R	O	T	G	B	M	P	E	N	A
V	S	O	P	R	A	Y	E	R	H	A	M	M	U	T
I	Q	F	T	H	R	O	N	E	D	L	O	G	E	W
W	J	S	E	C	I	F	I	R	C	A	S	A	W	T

Bonus Trivia

In what city is the world's largest Protestant church (numerically) located?

Seoul, South Korea.

43

21

Joy Shirk

Jesus' "I Am" Statements*

BREAD OF LIFE	Lord of the SABBATH
CHRIST	MASTER
DOOR OF THE SHEEP	MESSIAH
GOOD SHEPHERD	RESURRECTION
JESUS Christ	SON OF GOD
Jesus of NAZARETH	SON OF MAN
LIFE	TRUE VINE
LIGHT OF THE WORLD	TRUTH
LIVING BREAD	WAY
LORD	

* Only find words in all capital letters.

```
N V Q H U K C Y H K C B E B C
O B G O O D S H E P H E R D P
I J S Q R J C L R Q F E E B E
T F H O O M E S S I A H T P E
C R L L N C S R T D S E S N H
E J U K J O P S O W F T A A S
R O Y E C H F F G I O H M Z E
R X S F V Y L M L E W I X A H
U U J K P I H T A B B A S R T
S D O G F O N O S N L Z H E F
E F Z E V L X E H H E T W T O
R W A Y P D Y I M A U Z L H R
J D L I V I N G B R E A D Z O
X B Z W J X R Z T L F H O T O
L I G H T O F T H E W O R L D
```

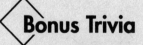

Bonus Trivia

What minor Bible character is the hymn
"Almost Persuaded" written about?

Agrippa.

22

Robert F. Dougherty

The Barren Fig Tree Cursed
(Matthew 21:17-22)

ANSWERED	JESUS
ASK	LEAVES
AWAY	MARVELLED
BELIEVING	MORNING
BETHANY	MOUNTAIN
CAME	NOTHING
CAST	ONLY
CITY	PRESENTLY
DISCIPLES	RECEIVE
DONE	REMOVED
DOUBT	RETURNED
EVER	SAID
FAITH	SAYING
FIG	SEA
FRUIT	SOON
GROW	THINGS
HAVE	WHATSOEVER
HENCEFORWARD	WITHERED
HUNGERED	

```
H R E M O V E D N O T H I N G
E M A C S S E D A W H B A Z U
N M P A G N E D H G I T U V N
C U I R R R E A M D N P I O E
E D O U E R T A R I G I O A D
F W T H E S R D T S S Y W F
O E T W O V E M G C A S T A A
R I S E E R O N T I U R F Y S
W N V L E U E K T P F A P Y K
A E L G N I V E I L E B Y I E
R E N T C J I F F E Y R S I P
D U A I O Y E D R S E V A E L
H I T S B D C S Y L N O N V U
N Y N A H T E B U L I O K E U
T A G N I N R O M S D Y E R F
```

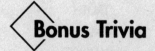

Bonus Trivia

What is the Tetragrammaton?

The sacred Hebrew name for God.

47

23

Robert F. Dougherty

Christ Walks on the Sea
(Matthew 14:26-33)

AFRAID

ANSWERED

BEGINNING

BOISTEROUS

CAUGHT

CEASED

CHEER

CRIED

DISCIPLES

DOWN

FAITH

FEAR

FORTH

GOD

GOOD

HAND

HEAR

IMMEDIATELY

JESUS

LITTLE

LORD

PETER

SAID

SAYING

SEA

SHIP

SPAKE

SPIRIT

STRAIGHTWAY

STRETCHED

THEM

TROUBLED

TRUTH

WALKED

WALKING

WATER

WERE

WORSHIPPED

```
S T R A I G H T W A Y E G P S
T A N S W E R E D L I T T L E
R S J B O I S T E R O U S I A
E P E T E R A T P T I R I P S
T A S R E T A W P H T R O F C
C K U G N I N N I G E B F H H
H E S C D T W H H U M M E T F
E Y S E C M A A S A T E A U D
D U M A L S L N R C R H R R A
P M D S Y P K D O E O T O T W
I B O E H I I N W D U L N A C
N W O D O A N C O F B P L R Q
M Q G H R W G G S X L K I U E
K Q U F A I T H Z I E E U H V
H E A R L C S A I D D D Z L S
```

◇ **Bonus Trivia**

What was the last book generally accepted as part of the New Testament?

2 Peter.

24

Robert F. Dougherty

The Woman Healed by Touching Christ's Garment
(Matthew 9:20–22)

ABOUT	ISSUE
BEHIND	JESUS
BEHOLD	MADE
BLOOD	MAY
BUT	SAID
CAME	SAW
COMFORT	SHALL
DAUGHTER	SHE
DISEASED	THY
FAITH	TOUCH
FEW	TOUCHED
FROM	TURNED
GARMENT	TWELVE
GOOD	WAS
HEM	WHEN
HER	WHICH
HERSELF	WHOLE
HIM	WITHIN
HIS	WOMAN
HOUR	YEARS

```
J D G F R M A D E H C U O T L
Y A M A W H I C H P S C W R T
B U H E R S E L F A A E I O L
E G J Y E M X B I M L N U F S
H H E A H R E D E V I C W M P
I T S R A E Y N E H H H A O P
N E U S S I W J T N O F S C L
D R S G A W H I M L R L T W A
O P U O F E W M E O L U D H M
O N T O M E L O M Z O A T E Y
L U K D H M V W M B N I H N X
B S R S X M Q X A A A G M S T
W S F D O P F E K F N W A S H
T Y R O C I O J Q X C M G I U
K T I R G P V C Q P N K C H U
```

◇ **Bonus Trivia**

What hymn were the passengers on the
Titanic reportedly singing as it went down?

"Nearer, My God, to Thee."

25

Dawna Cramer

Jewels and Gems

AMETHYST	JASPER
BERYL	JEWEL
BRACELETS	NECKLACE
CHAIN	NOSE RINGS
CHALCEDONY	ONYX
CHRYSOLITE	PEARLS
CHRYSOPRASUS	PRECIOUS
CORAL	QUARTZ
CRYSTAL	RUBY
DIAMOND	SAPPHIRE
EMERALD	SARDINE STONE
GEM	SARDIUS
GOLD	SARDONYX
IVORY	SILVER
JACINTH	TOPAZ

```
T O P A Z E T I L O S Y R H C
D X Y N O D R A S I L V E R M
N S W O J A C I N T H P D F Z
E R G E M H H R H G D Y O S S
C N W N A S A W Y P T M S U A
K E K I I W L L V S P Y S O R
L M N V C R C E K Y T A T I D
A E N O T S E N I D R A S C I
C R R R A H D S H P S R L E U
E A E Y U R O I O R E E Y R S
L L Q G X B N S A N E A B P V
U D A H H E Y D L M Y P R G D
G O R Z T R A U Q N O X S L Y
A M E T H Y S T M X Z N O A S
B R A C E L E T S X H G D V J
```

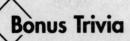

Bonus Trivia

What did President Reagan declare 1983 the year of?

The Bible.

26

Dawna Cramer

The Armor of God

ARMOR	PRINCIPALITIES
BREASTPLATE	QUENCH
DARKNESS	RIGHTEOUSNESS
DARTS	RULERS
DEVIL	SALVATION
FAITH	SHIELD
FEET	SHOD
GOD	SPIRIT
GOSPEL	STAND
HELMET	STRONG
LOINS	SWORD
LORD	TRUTH
MIGHT	WHOLE
PEACE	WILES
POWERS	WORD

```
R S H O D L E C A E P T R B T
Q U E N C H M U S T R A D T U
E W L H T N E A T U I V R Q M
L U M E G N O R T S N R F F R
O O E H R B E H E J C O I O Z
H F T J M S W O R D I X M P W
W F A I T H W O R D P R J G S
S A L V A T I O N R A X S F T
L U P O X B L J I R L H K V B
L W T H I Y E S F L I V E D D
E M S S E N S U O E T H G I R
P Z A Z F G S F L M I H I P G
S S E N K R A D L A E Q G J M
O W R K M P O W E R S N S I O
G D B T N G U R D N A T S L M
```

◇ **Bonus Trivia**

What brush with death made Martin Luther
decide to become a monk?

He was struck by lightning.

27

Dawna Cramer

The Ten Commandments

ADULTERY

ALTAR

COVET

FALSE

FATHER

GRAVEN IMAGE

HOLY

HONOUR

HOUSE

I AM

JEALOUS

KILL

LIGHTNINGS

LORD

MAIDSERVANT

MANSERVANT

MOSES

MOTHER

MOUNT SINAI

NAME

NEIGHBOR

NO OTHER GODS

PEOPLE

REST

SABBATH

SACRIFICE

STEAL

THUNDERINGS

TRUMPET

VAIN

WIFE

WITNESS

```
M Y S R J E A L O U S T N L M
A F A E A R D A L T A R L I O
N N C H T H U N D E R I N G S
S E R T R O L D P X K D R H E
E I I O N K T R P H L A E T S
R A F M O C E R O O V A I N S
V N I X O H R L U E W Y V I E
A I C V T B Y E N O W W R N N
N S E A H G T I S H N L O G T
T T F T E P M U R T H O B S I
I N O S R A Y J C A D R H K W
V U U B G U P I R B F D G U I
I O P E O P L E O B G B I S F
H M A I D S E R V A N T E A E
V F A L S E M A N S A Q N H M
```

◇ Bonus Trivia

What was unusual about the albums of
contemporary Christian singer Keith Green?

He sold them for whatever people said
they could afford.

28

Dawna Cramer

Heaven

ALPHA

ANGELS

BOOK

CROWNS

ELDERS

ETERNAL

GATES

GLORY

GOD

GOLD

HEAVEN

JASPER

JEWELS

LAMB OF GOD

LAMP

LIGHT

MANSION

NO CRYING

NO DEATH

NO PAIN

NO SORROW

OMEGA

PEARLY GATES

SAINTS

SEALS

SEA OF GLASS

THRONE

TREE OF LIFE

WATER OF LIFE

WORSHIP

WORTHY

```
N V N N S L E W E J N S G N N
E X S R U K R W M A N S I O N
V T N S S T N I A S F U S C F
A H P L A G A I K P I O N R G
E R G X M L E L D E R S E Y E
H O S E T A G Y L R A E P I F
W N L H D O G F O B M A L N I
P E E O H S N W O R C J A G L
S O G J T S N O P A I N N A F
E D N W A O K R T E E D R A O
T W A S E A L S H D U S E S R
A T W P D G M H L I G H T K E
G V M S O E F I L F O E E R T
X A F L N M O P Z U D U E F A
L P D Y R O L G N Y H T R O W
```

⟨**Bonus Trivia**

How is church music sung if it is done "a cappella"?

Without instruments.

29

Dawna Cramer

Kings

ABIJAM	JEROBOAM
AHAB	JOSIAH
AHAZIAH	JOTHAM
AMAZIAH	MANASSEH
AMON	MENAHEM
ASA	NADAB
AZARIAH	OMRI
BAASHA	PEKAH
DAVID	PEKAHIAH
HAZAEL	REHOBOAM
HEZEKIAH	SAUL
JEHOAHAZ	SHALLUM
JEHOASH	SOLOMON
JEHORAM	ZECHARIAH
JEHU	ZIMRI

```
J G V U P L H M D E S W H Z H
E E G H A K E P T S V A E E A
H A R J H N Z I M R I L S C I
O E M E A E E L K S X S U H H
R H I H B S K I O Z A C N A A
A D E U A O I J S N B E Q R K
M M U N H L A Z A R I A H I E
L M A S S O H M U X J F T A P
J O T H A M A Z L E A Z A H M
V F X G A O Z M H V M L M Z U
Z V W T B N I O F O O W A N L
I R M O A K A O D C N O Z S L
Z Z H T F S H D A V I D I G A
S E J E H O A H A Z X W A I H
R G E B H Z J R B B I R H M S
```

61

30

Alice Rafidi

King David's Family

ABIGAIL	JESSE
ABITAL	JESUS
ABSALOM	JOAB
AHINOAM	JONADAB
AMASA	MAACAH
AMNON	MICHAL
ASAHEL	NATHAN
BATHSHEBA	NOGAH
BOAZ	OBED
DAVID	OZEM
EGLAH	RADDAI
ELIADA	RUTH
ELIHU	SHIMEA
ELISHAMA	SHOBAB
HAGGITH	SOLOMON
IBHAR	TAMAR
ITHREAM	ZERUIAH
JAPHIA	

```
N A M N O N E E L I S H A M A
O F A A Z O Z L G L E H A S A
M K E T E V M A I L D E K Z J
O Y R H N A K A J H A I Q O O
L Z H A O U D T A B U H A T N
O E T N G D D I Z C Z B V I A
S K I R A I U D I V A D U L D
O H A R H R J R I T B H W A A
A S U S E J A Z H M I T N H B
B H O Z E M P S U B T I J C A
I I G S R R H L Z T A G G I O
G M S E O E I P A A L G Q M I
A E C A B S A L O M R A H B I
I A O A E S H O B A B H T U R
L Y P A D A I L E R A M A S A
```

Bonus Trivia

What flower is used as a mnemonic device by seminary students to remember the five points of Calvinism?

Tulip.

31

Alice Rafidi

Jesus & John the Baptist

ANGEL	JOSEPH
BABE	JOY
BAPTIZE	LORD
BLESSED	MANGER
BLOOD	MARY
CALL	PEACE
COUSINS	PRIEST
CRUCIFY	REPENT
DOVE	SACRIFICE
ELISABETH	SALVATION
FORGIVENESS	SAVED
GABRIEL	SINS
GLORY	SON
GOD	SOUL
GREAT	STAR
HAIL	THE WAY
HAND	THRONE
HATH	TIME
HEARTS	VISION
HEROD	WATER
HIS	WOMB
HOLY GHOST	WORD
JESUS	ZACHARIAS

```
H M M B S G A B R I E L U O S
Z O V J L D O V E N O R H T M
E H L O W O R D J B A A S H H
M A R Y Y R O U O T N E L E T
F Y U F G E R D S D I H L W E
O L L I A H P E E R A M A A B
R L X C J N O S P T D N C Y A
G C O U S I N S H E M O G J S
I F G R E A T E T S N I S E I
V L U C D W Y L E M I T H S L
E E Z I T P A B A B E A E U E
N C L R E G N A M D E V A S G
E A I D S V I S I O N L R L Z
S E C I F I R C A S W A T E R
S P W Z A C H A R I A S S U M
```

Bonus Trivia

After the Bible was divided into chapters, how many years passed before it was divided into verses?

300 (about A.D. 1250-1500).

32

Stephen Powers

People and Places
of Acts 1

ACELDAMA	JUDAS
ANDREW	JUDAEA
APOSTLES	MARY
BARSABAS	MATTHEW
BARTHOLOMEW	MATTHIAS
DAVID	OLIVET
GALILEE	PETER
HEAVEN	PHILIP
ISRAEL	SAMARIA
JAMES	SIMON
JERUSALEM	THEOPHILUS
JESUS	THOMAS
JOHN	UPPER ROOM
JOSEPH	

```
G W M O O R R E P P U N R Q H
M E I R S A I H T T A M E B P
A R T S A D U J R U I J T A E
R D B W M D N O M I S V E A S
Y N A Z P R G T M A M A P M O
B A R T H O L O M E W I H A J
B X S H I M C A S D I E I D E
R V A E Y C R I P A A B L L R
O I B O A I O L I V E T I E E
K S A P A Q Q S E I A V P C S
A R S H D Q J N Y D D L G A A
G A L I L E E N R D U A M O L
Y E G L M I S E M A J O H N E
W L D U E F U T W E H T T A M
O Q Q S O N S E L T S O P A Q
```

◇ Bonus Trivia

What are the two major branches of the
Orthodox Church?

Greek and Russian.

33

Evelyn M. Boyington

Men Called by God to Special Service

AARON	JAMES
ABRAHAM	JOHN
AMOS	JONAH
APOLLOS	JOSEPH
BARAK	JOSHUA
DANIEL	JUDE
DAVID	MARK
EHUD	MOSES
ELIJAH	NOAH
ELISHA	PETER
EZEKIEL	PHILIP
EZRA	SAMUEL
GIDEON	SAUL
HOSEA	SILAS
ISAAC	STEPHEN
ISAIAH	TIMOTHY
JACOB	

```
C W A R Z E G D M S C E Z S N
T B S H L B C E I A D D T P J
K S E I A W V D A V D U H E X
A S S R R J C S E M A J D C E
R H O T R R I G S B Y D R H F
A E M S E A H L R O H P E U E
B B T C A P S A E E T J M Z K
Z O N E E L H A C U O X E O V
O C Z S P A I E U H M K K S J
L A O X M G P S N L I A I O A
P J O N A H L O R E T C S M D
N O E D I G R H L C A H A A E
S L V L M A R K S L U A I W U
L E I N A D Y E H A O N A O I
F P P R P I F P V Y D S H O U
```

◇ **Bonus Trivia**

In "Beneath the Cross of Jesus," there are "two wonders I confess." What are they?

Christ's love and my unworthiness.

34

Evelyn M. Boyington

Prophecies Fulfilled
by Jesus

AROSE	NAZARENE
ASCEND	PARABLES
BETHLEHEM	PIERCED
BETRAYED	PRIEST
CORNERSTONE	REJECTED
CRUCIFIED	RULE
DAVID	SAD
EGYPT	SAVE
EMMANUEL	SCEPTER
ETERNAL	SCOURGED
FORSAKEN	SPIRIT
GIFTS	THIRST
GOD	THRONE
HEAL	VIRGIN
HIGH	WORSHIP
JUDAH	ZEAL

```
M D F D P T K S T H R O N E V
P E E O E I S D T L S A V E I
S A H Y R C H E I F A S A D R
Y C R E A S R S I V I E R D G
Y L O A L R A E R R A G H C I
A A T U B H T K I O P D O L N
D E H D R L T E E P W R E V R
E Z I N G G E E B N N U E E A
I T R E O J E S B E N N J L S
F I S L D N T D R A E E A C D
I R T U C H E S M R C N E N E
C I Z R A G T M A T R P E S H
U P U D Y O E Z E E T C O I T
R S U P N V A D T E S R G P T
C J T E V N I E R A A H B A K
```

◁ **Bonus Trivia**

In Dante's *Inferno,* who are held by Satan in
the deepest pit?

Judas, Cassius, and Brutus (for being
traitors).

71

35

Evelyn M. Boyington

Cities of Defeated Kings
(Joshua 12)

ACHSHAPH

ADULLAM

AI

APHEK

ARAD

BETHEL

DEBIR

DOR

EGLON

GEDER

GEZER

GILGAL

HAZOR

HEBRON

HEPHER

HORMAH

JARMUTH

JERICHO

JERUSALEM

JOKNEAM

KEDESH

LACHISH

LASHARON

LIBNAH

MADON

MAKKEDAH

MEGIDDO

SHIMRON-MERON

TAANACH

TAPPUAH

TIRZAH

```
I V X W L E H T E B P H H V G
H H A U P P A T L F A O U E Q
F S M P G H A H U D R O Z A H
N L I E H A W R E M A E G C D
R O D H N E T K A H R M K M G
D E R A C O K H Y P A A E X R
R S C E R A R L A A D L J R T
W H X F M I L B A H A L A L N
M S T L E N B J E S K U D O G
M E G I D D O E U H H D D I E
Q D Q B R M L R D C J A L G G
W E T N T Z E I M A M G R X L
P K W A L J A C J I A H Q O O
H E P H E R W H X L H V G J N
B F M A E N K O J U T S W N Y
```

Bonus Trivia

What version of the Bible became the
surprise runaway bestseller of the mid 1960s?

The Living Bible.

36

Evelyn M. Boyington

Commerce in the Bible

APPAREL	LEAD
BRASS	LINEN
BUYING	MARITIME
CARAVAN	MERCHANDISE
CATTLE	MERCHANTS
CHAPMEN	OIL
CHARIOTS	PERFUME
CHESTS	PURPLE
CLOTH	SELLING
CORN	SILVER
EMBROIDERY	SLAVES
FAIRS	STEEL
GEMS	TIN
GOLD	TRADE
HONEY	TRAFFIC
IRON	WARES
IVORY	WINE
LAND	WOOL

```
E Z S R I A F C H E S T S D J
U S P M H T O L C L E S L N A
S D I E E L C I T L E A A H Y
H L R D R G F H P R N V V R E
X O O J N F C R A D A R E E N
C G N E A A U W E R M D S V O
F N N R N P H M A L I O E L H
W I T B W I I C E O E O M I H
L L O O W T W C R L E E T S Z
L L G N I Y U B O E V J V S C
A E D R R P M Q M R M H K A J
G S A O M E R C H A N T S R G
D M V D Q K T O S P J C I B F
F I U B G I N E M P A H C N H
L H G C H Q G P C A T T L E N
```

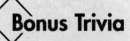

Bonus Trivia

Early Christians sometimes met in
catacombs. What are catacombs?

Cemeteries.

37

Sally K. Morrison

Men of the Bible

AARON	ISSACHAR
ABEL	JACOB
ABRAHAM	JARED
ABSALOM	JESSE
ADAM	JETHRO
ASHER	JOSEPH
BENJAMIN	JOSHUA
BOAZ	JUDAH
CALEB	LEVI
DAN	MANASSEH
DAVID	MOSES
ELI	NAPHTALI
ELIEZER	NOAH
ELIJAH	PAUL
ENOCH	REHOBOAM
EPHRAIM	SAMSON
GAD	SAMUEL
GERSHOM	SAUL
ISHMAEL	SIMEON
ISAAC	ZEBULUN

```
W I Z E I B G A D S I M E O N
L U A P D B E E A Z A U A A U
J E T H R O R M A U S B P M L
E L S R J A S S H Z E H J E U
S I B A J O H S T L T L K L B
S E T I N E O E N A A V M E E
E Z V M R J M O L A S B A U Z
E E D A N A A I D F M E O M C
L R I H D H N F I B B N B A I
I S S A C H A R V R J J O S R
J J A R T O S G A U O A H H Y
A A A B V L S U D S A M E C Z
H O C A A U E A E R A I R O A
S E S O M A H P O E L N M N O
C A L E B S H N L E U B O E B
```

Bonus Trivia

Complete this Peter Marshall quote:
"Today's Christians are too often like deep-sea divers. . .

marching bravely forth to pull plugs out of bathtubs."

77

38

Sally K. Morrison

Women of the Bible

ABIGAIL	MAACAH
ASENATH	MARTHA
AZUBAH	MARY
BASEMATH	MICHAL
BATHSHEBA	MIRIAM
DEBORAH	NAOMI
DINAH	PRISCILLA
DORCAS	RACHEL
ELIZABETH	RUTH
ESTHER	SAPPHIRA
EVE	SARAH
HAGAR	SUSANNA
HANNAH	TAMAR
HELAH	TIMNA
HERODIAS	ZILPAH
JOANNA	ZIPPORAH
LEAH	

```
H A N N A H T A N E S A B J X
M I C H A L R T N A H T R A M
S A P P H I R A A N N A S U S
M K L A R A U H C T A D F D A
S I E X N I G S A H M O J O I
Z L R M L D S A S C E B J R D
I K I I H A C R H A L Z C O
P T J N A Q N B I S T A M A R
P A A D G M I L E L E U M S E
O H J S I E H M B H L N R V H
R B F X B Z A A O M S A E H A
A N W K A T G R Y A Y H H E R
H L S O H U C Y V Y N O T L A
D E B O R A H A B U Z A S A S
W Y X V H T E B A Z I L E H B
```

◇ **Bonus Trivia**

What kind of Christian organization is
"AIA"?

A basketball team (Athletes in Action).

39

Arlene Walker

A Virtuous Woman
(Proverbs 31:9-31)

BEAUTY	LOINS
BUYETH	MAIDENS
CANDLE	MERCHANDISE
CHILDREN	NEEDY
CLOTHING	NIGHT
DISTAFF	OPEN
FIELD	PORTION
FOOD	PRAISETH
FRUIT	PRICE
GATES	PURPLE
GIVETH	RUBIES
GOOD	SCARLET
HANDS	SPINDLE
HER	STRENGTH
HONOUR	TAPESTRY
HOUSEHOLD	THOU
HUSBAND	VAIN
LIFE	WILLINGLY
LINEN	

```
B Q F W I L L I N G L Y U F Y
H U L I F E L P R U P H R T N
G A Y E E Y D E E N O U U E C
H A N E S L N A V U I A N Y L
T S T D T I D O S T E I E R O
E E H E S H D E I B L N C T T
S I G G S R H N D T N E I S H
I B I O U O F M A N R P R E I
A U N O L F A S S H A O P P N
R R N D A I C C G P C B P A G
P O O T D A A S R I I R S T U
H O S E R N R N I A V N E U O
F I N L D E S N I O L E D M H
D S E L H T G N E R T S T L T
K T E B Q N E R D L I H C H E
```

◇ Bonus Trivia

What article of clothing was the trademark of
Christian poet Helen Steiner Rice?

Floppy hats.

81

40

Arlene Walker

Seven

ABOMINATIONS	MONTHS
ALTARS	NATIONS
ANGELS	OXEN
BASKETS	PILLARS
BRETHREN	PLAGUES
BULLOCKS	PRINCES
CANDLESTICKS	SABBATHS
CHURCHES	SEALS
CUBITS	SHEPHERDS
DAUGHTERS	SONS
HORNS	SOULS
HUNDRED	STARS
LAMBS	TIMES
LAMPS	TRIBES
LOCKS	VIALS
MAIDENS	WEEKS

```
A H S C S K C O L L U B A S A
S L O P A T R I B E S B B N L
S E T R M N Y N E X O M G O S
H P A A N A D O J M A E C O S
E R W L R S L L I L L K U V A
P I E K S S N E S S L V I B
H N E F W E A B B S S O I A B
E C K X U T R H M A T T N L A
R E S G I E U N S A S I A S T
D S A O T N A S C R I K C R H
S L N H D T H J M U A D E K S
P S R R I T E D R L B L E T S
L E E O N W S E M I T I L N S
N D N O C H U R C H E S T I S
Z S M D S R E T H G U A D S P
```

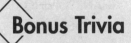

Bonus Trivia

What is the longest book of the New Testament?

ʇuke.

41

Arlene Walker

Prayer

AFFLICTED	GLORIFY
ALONE	GODS WILL
ALWAYS	HUMBLE
ASK	KNEEL
BELIEVE	KNOCK
CALL	MERCY
CLEANSE	PEACE
CLOSET	PETITION
CONTINUE	PURIFY
CRY	SECRET
DELIVERANCE	SEEK
DESIRE	SING
EVERYTHING	SUPPLICATIONS
EXALT	THANK
FAITH	THANKSGIVING
FAST	TOGETHER
FORGIVE	WATCH

```
T E F L L I W S D O G L S B F
G E L A W A T C H B E N E O P
M T S B I F A S T E O L R U G
A E H O M T I M N I I G R T N
F P R A L U H K T E I I A O I
F E K C N C H A V V F S K G H
L A C A Y K C E E Y K E G E T
I C O L L I S E E T E R N T Y
C E N L L D G G U S E S I H R
T W K P E S E L I N N R S E E
E W P S Y X D J O V I A C R V
D U I A A L O N E R I T E E E
S R W L R K N A H T I N N L S
E L T N O I T I T E P F G O C
A E C N A R E V I L E D Y R C
```

Bonus Trivia

Due to a misprint, what "commandment" appeared in the "Wicked Bible" of 1641?

Thou shalt commit adultery.

42

Arlene Walker

Neighbors and Enemies
(Proverbs 25:8-28)

APPLES	NITRE
BROKEN	OBEDIENT
CLOUDS	ORNAMENT
COUNTENANCE	PICTURES
DEBATE	RAIN
DISCOVER	REPROVER
END	SECRET
FALSE	SHAME
FOOT	SILVER
GOOD NEWS	SNOW
HARVEST	SOFT
HASTILY	SONGS
HATE	SPOKEN
HONEY	STRIVE
HOUSE	TURN
JOINT	VINEGAR
LEST	WALLS
MAUL	WEATHER
MESSENGER	WITHDRAW

```
R S C Y T N E M A N R O F R B
N A E O E E V I R T S A E R E
R E G L U N M A U L L G O T H
U R K E P N O E E S N K A O W
T E S O N P T H E E B U O A
N P H F P I A E S N E S N S R
E R A O W S V S N D E S I G D
I O M O G R E D H A J I A N H
D V E T E M I Y W A N O R O T
E E H V W S L E T C R C I S I
B R L A C I A T S E L V E N W
O I L O T T F O S Q R O E N T
S L V S H E E R T I N C U S D
S E A E S E R U T C I P E D T
R H R T D S W E N D O O G S S
```

◇ **Bonus Trivia**

What British poet first commented that God did not make woman out of man's head to be over him or out of man's foot to be under him but out of man's rib to be beside him?

Geoffrey Chaucer (in *The Canterbury Tales*).

43

J's in the Bible

Betty Leavitt

JACOB	JEZEBEL
JAIRUS	JOAB
JAMES	JOASH
JAPHETH	JOB
JEHOIACHIN	JOEL
JEHOSHAPHAT	JOHN
JEHU	JONATHAN
JEREMIAH	JOSEPH
JERICHO	JOSHUA
JERUSALEM	JOSIAH
JESSE	JOY
JESUS	JUDAS
JETHRO	JUDE

```
J  M  J  E  R  I  C  H  O  O  S  E  M  A  J
P  E  E  M  J  P  A  S  N  J  O  B  P  E  O
L  L  H  X  O  J  B  U  C  E  E  H  Z  H  A
P  A  U  O  A  R  Z  R  T  S  J  E  G  A  B
K  S  M  L  S  V  X  I  W  S  B  X  Y  I  X
N  U  U  K  H  H  T  A  Q  E  H  B  R  S  X
I  R  R  Y  C  Q  A  J  L  A  U  H  S  O  J
H  E  A  O  T  S  G  P  I  S  Q  S  Y  J  N
C  J  A  J  A  W  H  M  H  L  B  I  T  A  D
A  Z  F  D  C  T  E  H  B  A  D  G  H  L  Q
I  A  U  L  E  R  J  P  B  T  T  T  B  E  B
O  J  Z  H  E  W  U  E  P  V  A  N  B  O  O
H  P  P  J  E  D  N  S  J  N  I  T  H  J  C
E  A  N  C  N  H  U  O  O  W  F  W  B  O  A
J  E  S  U  S  R  A  J  L  O  R  H  T  E  J
```

◇ Bonus Trivia

What is the Authorized Version of the Bible called in the United States?

The King James Version.

44

Betty Leavitt

Isaiah's Pictures of Jesus Christ

BURDEN BEARER	MIGHTY GOD
COMPASSION	PREACHER
GENTLE	PRINCE OF PEACE
IMMANUEL	REPROVER
INTERCESSOR	RIGHTEOUS KING
JUDGE	SAVIOUR
JUST	SERVANT
LAWGIVER	SIN-BEARER
LIBERATOR	SINLESS
MEEK	WISE

```
M I G H T Y G O D M H O O P S
S E R V A N T L E U N A M M I
G F E T M C O M P A S S I O N
N I P C S L R O T A R E B I L
I N R E A P Z D H O B N V L E
K E O J V E O B S L M I A Y S
S K V H I X P S X E M W U I S
U K E J O K E F S E G S N Z R
O E R S U C V N O I T B V S E
E E M R R D T E V E E A V H H
T M C E B S G E L A C G H L C
H R T K U E R E R T E N Y G A
G N H J K N L E F B N B I D E
I X W I S E R S J I N E K R R
R E R A E B N E D R U B G S P
```

Bonus Trivia

What Shakespearian play is considered his most "Christian" for its resurrection and redemption images?

Measure for Measure.

45

Betty Leavitt

Buildings and Dwellings

ARK	HOUSE
BOOTH	PALACE
BULRUSHES	PARADISE
CASTLES	SYNAGOGUE
CAVES	TABERNACLE
CITIES OF REFUGE	TEMPLE
DEN	TENTS
FORTRESS	TOWER OF BABEL
HEAVEN	WILDERNESS

```
E C A L A P Z B S W T U K R A
A E X W X P E U S E O L Z F C
D H P Q L H U L E G W R G G M
C A V E S C G R N U E J Q H N
P I E A W E O U R F R X P L B
H E A V E N G S E E O F E J O
R G T O G S A H D R F Y L T V
H W E V R M N E L F B S C M P
O X N O N B Y S I O A S A W S
U W T P S C S V W S B E N F E
S Y S K H D D O D E E R R G L
E I O T S I E V P I L T E Q T
J F O B P P F N O T P R B X S
R O Z T E M P L E I C O A E A
B P A R A D I S E C C F T N C
```

◇ Bonus Trivia

What unusual decision stimulated John
Fawcett to write "Blest Be the Tie That
Binds"?

He turned down the pastorate of a larger
church with a bigger salary.

46

Betty Leavitt

Music

CORNET	PSALTERIES
CYMBALS	RAMS HORNS
DULCIMER	SACKBUT
FLUTE	SINGERS
HARP	TABRETS
HYMNS	TIMBREL
ORGAN	TRUMPETS
PIPE	VIOL
PSALMS	

```
H B E R E M I C L U D B K Y C
S Y I X S J O V T R U X M Y O
T N M S I N G E R S N V M F R
B O A N G O L K Y C V B D C N
A U N P S L O I V X A V C H E
J P V I O W J U F L G T A D T
T I T A B R E T S A A R I D O
R Y B A L V I M L A P R S E K
U G O L P S E I R E T L A S P
M P O E W S R O G J Z V C X I
P A I R I D A A R T E V K D P
E O R B G L F L U T E M B F E
T F D M N A N G M N L I U Y P
S D R I B X N B L S U N T Q Q
Q W M T M T S N R O H S M A R
```

Bonus Trivia

What did Muhammed-ad-Dhib find in a cave in 1947?

The Dead Sea Scrolls.

47

Kerri Irwin

Route of the Exodus to the Promised Land

EGYPT	KADESH-BARNEA
RAAMSES	MT HOR
SUCCOTH	EZION GEBER
ETHAM	ZIN WILDERNESS
RED SEA	NEGEB
MARAH	EDOM
ELIM	MOAB
REPHIDIM	MT NEBO
MT SINAI	PISGAH
HOREB	JERICHO

```
X Z O S Y S W B U W H O R E B
I K I U I A N I S T M F U V I
J O Q K E K C B O I Y X Z R T
R M Z E B A H A D B R I S A R
M E I U D G A I B G N G E A J
P V D L A O H Q J W Q N Z M D
I B I S E P M D I H R E I S S
M T Y W E L L L T A M G O E V
B O M R G A D O B F R E N S P
T Y A W Y E C H P O U B G B I
D H H B R C S O H C I R E J S
J E T N U E Z T I H V H B W G
I F E S D Y M G T P Y G E T A
F S H A Z I W O I O M A R A H
S O K B M T N E B O A N O P D
```

Bonus Trivia

The oldest partial New Testament
manuscript is a portion of the Gospel of John.
What is this manuscript's approximate date?

A.D. 130.

48

Kerri Irwin

Ordinary Objects Used by God in the Bible

DONKEY	LOINCLOTH
DUST	OIL
FIVE LOAVES BREAD	PIGS
FLEECE	POTTERY
FLIES	RAIN
FOOD	RIVERS
FROGS	ROD
HAIL	SLING
IRON PLATE	SMALL STONE
JARS	TORCHES
JAWBONE	TRUMPETS
LICE	TWO FISH
LOCUSTS	WATER

S	J	T	G	H	S	H	T	S	U	D	L	I	C	E
R	L	Q	S	T	E	P	M	U	R	T	U	F	E	V
T	P	I	G	S	W	Y	K	Q	V	A	L	I	F	B
W	R	X	N	L	A	X	Y	V	I	I	J	T	O	Y
O	B	S	O	G	T	R	V	R	E	B	H	R	D	Y
F	R	O	G	S	E	V	I	S	T	S	U	C	O	L
I	B	G	L	T	R	N	J	M	K	R	S	W	F	D
S	C	B	T	E	Z	L	W	A	E	Y	A	L	D	T
H	T	O	L	C	N	I	O	L	W	P	F	I	F	O
A	P	S	R	E	V	I	R	L	Y	B	X	Y	N	R
L	X	D	O	E	Q	G	I	S	Q	E	O	H	J	C
C	I	W	D	L	F	A	S	T	F	N	K	N	D	H
G	Q	O	I	F	H	B	U	O	H	D	Q	N	E	E
O	O	U	E	T	A	L	P	N	O	R	I	X	O	S
F	I	V	E	L	O	A	V	E	S	B	R	E	A	D

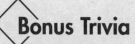

Bonus Trivia

"One short sleep past, we wake eternally, / And death shall be no more; death, thou shalt die." Who is the author of this sonnet?

John Donne.

49

Kerri Irwin

Cities in O. T. Israel (Divided Kingdom)

APHEK	KEDESH
BETHEL	MAHANAIM
BETHSHAN	MEDEBA
DAN	MEGIDDO
DIBON	PENUEL
GEZER	SAMARIA
HAZOR	SHECHEM
HESHBON	SHILOH
IBLEAM	SUCCOTH
JABESH-GILEAD	TAANACH
JERICHO	TIRZAH

```
L A G V K T L M S O Z A N U N
M E N G Y Y I M E U X T K A O
H G H L E A F R V G C H M F D
L S J T N Z T C Z D I C U N B
S A E A E A E A L A V D O O W
S X H D B B L R A A H B D T L
A A V E E F S N N I T R O H
M U D N Q K S X A D A O V Q V
I E S P O H T H L M Z C L J J
M B Y H E B S A G A A E H E G
A T L C X H H H H I U R R W K
H P H E T V R S I N L I I V E
W E H E A B P M E L C E T A Z
M S B E A M G P G H O N A F I
V Q R E K X W X O Y P H K D I
```

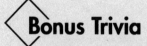

Bonus Trivia

What was Alexander Cruden noted for?

He put together a concordance to help
people find Bible verses.

50

Books in the New Testament

Kerri Irwin

MATTHEW	THESSALONIANS
MARK	TIMOTHY
LUKE	TITUS
JOHN'S GOSPEL	PHILEMON
ACTS	HEBREWS
ROMANS	JAMES
CORINTHIANS	PETER
GALATIANS	JOHN
EPHESIANS	JUDE
PHILIPPIANS	REVELATION
COLOSSIANS	

```
J Y S D K R V B Q N W I T D S
O Y H G U G E D S O E C D U C
H C P T S T S V U M H D T J O
N O T K O V N R E E T I X O L
P R I D W M A I X L T Z N H O
L I P H I L I P P I A N S N S
U N K B F E N T X H M T Z S S
P T J D K F O J M P Z T I G I
S H T U E Y L C H A R X F O A
N I L I Z B A V B Z R X J S N
A A S N A I S E H P E K X P S
M N D S W U S J A M E S I E Z
O S T V Z H E B R E W S G L J
R C V Y T U H R E T E P A E C
A S S N A I T A L A G J U D E
```

◇ Bonus Trivia

Southern gospel singer Christy Lane became
most famous for a song in which she pleads,
"Help me to pray, / Teach me to take, / . . ."
What?

"One day at a time."

103

Word Search Answers

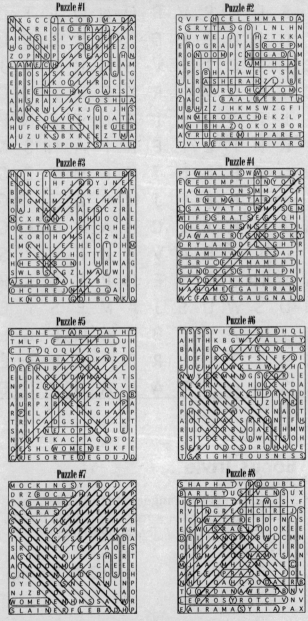

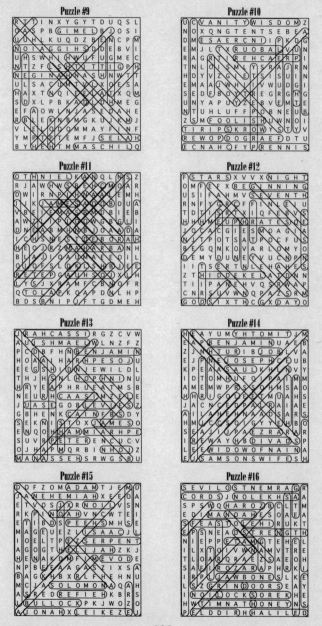

Puzzle #9

Puzzle #10

Puzzle #11

Puzzle #12

Puzzle #13

Puzzle #14

Puzzle #15

Puzzle #16

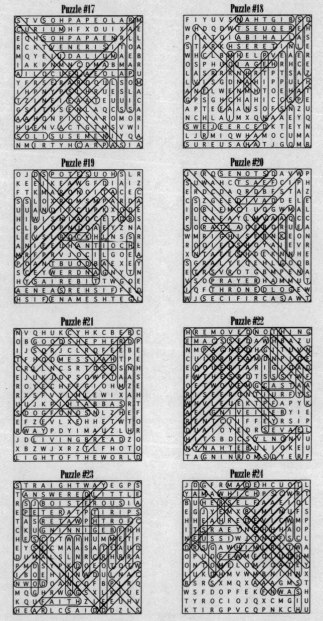

Puzzle #17

Puzzle #18

Puzzle #19

Puzzle #20

Puzzle #21

Puzzle #22

Puzzle #23

Puzzle #24

106

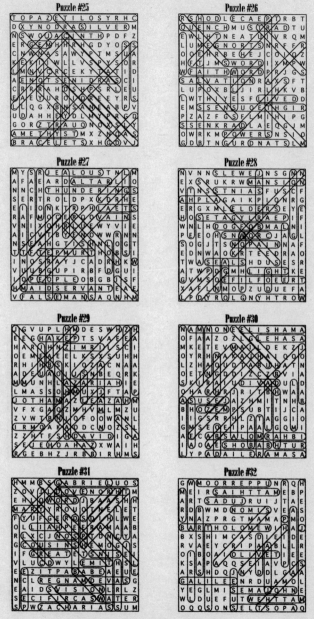

Puzzle #25

Puzzle #26

Puzzle #27

Puzzle #28

Puzzle #29

Puzzle #30

Puzzle #31

Puzzle #32

107

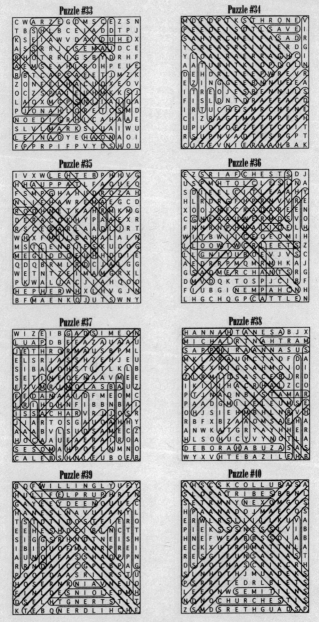

Puzzle #33

Puzzle #34

Puzzle #35

Puzzle #36

Puzzle #37

Puzzle #38

Puzzle #39

Puzzle #40

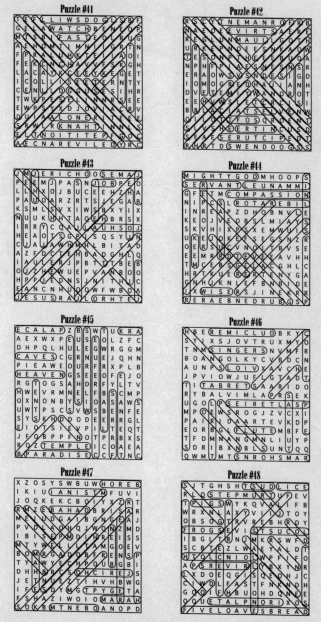

Puzzle #41

Puzzle #42

Puzzle #43

Puzzle #44

Puzzle #45

Puzzle #46

Puzzle #47

Puzzle #48

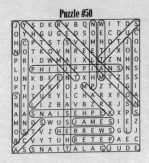